The Boston Massacre

by Marylou Morano Kjelle

Content Consultant
Robert J. Allison, Professor of History
Suffolk University

CORE
LIBRARY

Published by ABDO Publishing Company, PO Box 398166, Minneapolis, MN 55439. Copyright © 2013 by Abdo Consulting Group, Inc. International copyrights reserved in all countries. No part of this book may be reproduced in any form without written permission from the publisher. The Core Library™ is a trademark and logo of ABDO Publishing Company.

Printed in the United States of America, North Mankato, Minnesota
112012
012013

Editor: Blythe Hurley
Series Designer: Becky Daum

Cataloging-in-Publication Data
Kjelle, Marylou Morano.
 The Boston Massacre / Marylou Morano Kjelle.
   p. cm. -- (Foundations of our nation)
Includes bibliographical references and index.
ISBN 978-1-61783-706-7
1. Boston Massacre, 1770--Juvenile literature.   I. Title.
973.3/113--dc22

                                                  2012946535

Photo credits: Getty Images, cover, 1, 12; North Wind/North Wind Picture Archives, 4, 8, 14, 16, 18, 20, 22, 25, 27, 31, 33, 35, 36, 38, 40, 45; Public domain, 6; New York Public Library/Getty Images, 10; Dorling Kindersley/ Getty Images, 28

Cover: The Boston Massacre resulted in the deaths of five citizens on March 5, 1770.

CONTENTS

CHAPTER ONE

Violence Explodes on the Streets of Boston

An uneasy feeling hung over the streets of Boston on March 5, 1770. Anger between the citizens and the occupying British soldiers had been causing fights for months. British soldiers had been the target of the citizens' anger for nearly two years. So far there had not been any tragedies. That was about to change.

The Boston Massacre was a result of the fighting between the British soldiers and the citizens of Boston, Massachusetts.

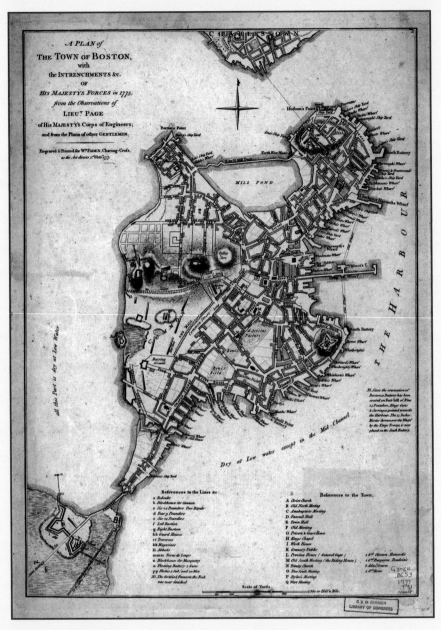

A Map of Boston during the 1770s

This is a map of Boston as it looked during the 1770s. How might a colonial city benefit by being surrounded by water? What might be some of the problems with such a location?

In 1770 there was one soldier for every four citizens in Boston. The soldiers were everywhere. They also stood guard at important buildings. One building was the Custom House. This building was under constant guard because important records and money were kept there.

The Mob Confronts the Soldier

Near the Custom House, an apprentice named Edward Garrick accused a British captain of not paying his master's bill. The guard standing nearby responded by hitting Garrick in the head with his gun. A mob gathered around the

George III: The Patriot King

With a reign of nearly 60 years, George III, the patriot king, was one of the longest ruling monarchs in English history. He was the first to use the term "mother country" when referring to Great Britain's relationship to the colonies. George believed he was a kind man who acted like a father to the colonies. He considered the colonies his children. The colonies were expected to obey their father. George hoped the colonies would give up their fight for independence.

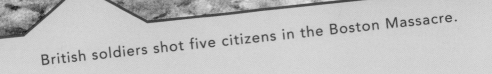

British soldiers shot five citizens in the Boston Massacre.

soldier. They trapped him against the door and threw rocks and chunks of ice at him. He responded by loading and pointing his gun.

Around the same time, the bells of Boston's churches and meeting halls began to ring. The ringing of bells was usually an alarm for fire. This time there was no fire. But many people ran out of their homes ready to help. Boston's narrow streets were blocked with hundreds of people.

Someone sent word to Boston's military headquarters that the soldier was in danger. Seven soldiers were ordered to march to his aid. But crowds blocked the way. The soldiers had to use their bayonets to poke their way through.

Blood on the Streets

The crowd was out of control by the time the soldiers reached the Custom House. The soldiers loaded their guns without being ordered to do so. British commanding officer Captain Thomas Preston begged the mob to go home. He tried to march his men back

Crispus Attucks was the first person killed in the Boston Massacre.

to their headquarters. But the soldiers were unable to move.

Someone in the crowd threw a club. It hit one of the soldiers in the head. He lost his balance and fell. His gun fired as he got up. Another soldier fired without aiming. Then the other soldiers fired as well.

Some of them later said they thought they had heard Preston give the command to fire.

Eleven colonists were hit by the gunfire. Three died instantly and another died a few hours later. Another survived for several days before dying. Six other people were wounded. None of the soldiers were killed or injured.

It would be five more years before the American colonists went to war to fight for their independence. But many colonists felt the men who lost their lives in the

Crispus Attucks

By some accounts, Crispus Attucks played a major role on the night of the Boston Massacre. An escaped slave, Attucks had been on the run for more than 20 years. At this time he worked as a seaman. Hearing the commotion, he led a group of colonists to the Custom House. Some witnesses said it was Attucks who threw the club that caused one of the soldiers to fall. As he rose, the soldier shot at Attucks' chest. Attucks was the first American to die in the quest for American independence.

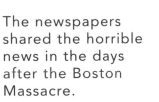

The newspapers shared the horrible news in the days after the Boston Massacre.

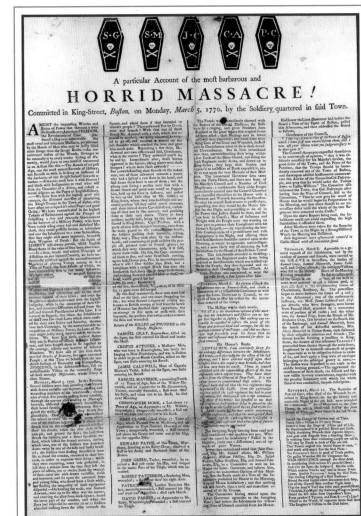

Boston Massacre were victims of the first battle of the Revolutionary War.

The Obituary of Patrick Carr

Patrick Carr was an Irish immigrant killed during the Boston Massacre. This notice was published in the *Boston Gazette*.

> *Last Wednesday night died, Patrick Carr, an Inhabitant of this Town, of the Wound he received . . . on the bloody and execrable Night of the 5th Instant.*
>
> *He had just before left his Home, and upon his coming into the Street received the fatal Ball in his Hip which passed out at the opposite Side . . . this is the fifth Life that has been sacrificed by the Rage of the Soldiery, but it is feared it will not be the last . . . His Remains were attended on Saturday last . . . to the same Grave, in which those who fell by the same Hands of Violence were interred the last Week.*
>
> Source: "Obituary of Patrick Carr." The Boston Gazette and Country Journal. March 19, 1770. Print.

Consider Your Audience

Read the passage above closely. How could you change this piece for a modern audience, such as your friends or classmates? Write a blog post sharing this same information with your new audience. What is the best way to get your point across to this audience? How is the language you use for your new audience different from the original text? Why?

CHAPTER TWO

Seeking Liberty

During the 1700s, Great Britain and France fought to become the most powerful country in the world. Both countries were heavily in debt by the time the fighting stopped. In North America, the conflict between Great Britain and France was known as the French and Indian War. Great Britain won the war, but it was very costly. The colonies needed a British army to keep the peace

The Stamp Act caused many riots in Boston.

Stamps Required by the Stamp Act

These were two of the stamps that had to be placed on printed materials under the Stamp Act. How are they the same as the stamps used on mail today? How are they different? Look at the design of the stamps. What about them might have made the colonists especially angry about having to use them?

between the colonists and American Indians. Great Britain felt the colonists should pay their fair share of these costs.

More Taxes for the Colonies

The British government decided creating more taxes would be a good way to earn money and control trade in the colonies. They passed a new tax called the Sugar Act in 1764. This made it cost more for the colonies to bring sugar and molasses into America. This act was followed a year later by the Stamp Act. This law taxed all printed documents. Newspapers, legal documents, and many other things had to have a stamp to show this tax had been paid. The colonists were more angry about this tax than any others that came before it. Past taxes had affected only a few people. But the Stamp Act affected all colonists.

Even more upsetting was that Great Britain was taxing the colonies without giving them any say in the matter. In Great Britain, citizens were represented by members of Parliament. The Boston colonists felt they deserved this right as well. "No taxation without representation" became their common cry.

The Colonists Take Action

A gathering called the Stamp Act Congress was held in New York City in October 1765. This gathering considered ways to protest this new law. A letter was sent to King George III saying the colonists disagreed

A dummy of Andrew Oliver was hung by protesting colonists.

with the tax. These actions did not influence the

British government. On November 1 the Stamp Act

became law.

Colonists in Massachusetts began fighting the Stamp Act in their own way. A group calling themselves the Loyal Nine and a mob of angry citizens destroyed a warehouse belonging to Andrew Oliver. His job was to enforce the Stamp Act in Massachusetts. The colonists also hung an effigy, or dummy, of Oliver from the Liberty Tree near Boston Common. Angry colonists followed this with other unlawful and sometimes violent acts.

Great Britain created a new series of laws called the Townshend Acts in 1767. These acts were created to control

The Sons of Liberty

In the early summer of 1765, a group of Boston men calling themselves the Loyal Nine began meeting in secret. They wanted to plan ways to fight the Stamp Act. Soon this group grew to include approximately 2,000 men. They called themselves the Sons of Liberty. By the end of the year, there were Sons of Liberty groups in every colony. They often used violence to spread their message. These groups made the first efforts to unite the colonies in preparation for war with Great Britain.

Colonists were required to provide food and shelter to British soldiers. This was part of the Quartering Act.

the colonists and raise taxes. These laws placed taxes on everyday items the colonists brought into America. This included tea, glass, paint, and paper. The Townshend Acts also gave British customs officials the power to search for and take away goods smuggled into the colonies. Some businesses had been smuggling goods in order to avoid paying taxes.

The Sons of Liberty planned boycotts, or agreements among colonists to not buy British goods. They also put pressure on merchants not to sell items made in Great Britain.

The British government began to see it would cost too much to carry out the Stamp Act. Parliament got rid of the act in early 1766. At the same time Parliament created a new law called the Declaratory Act. This law made it clear Great Britain had a right to make laws and pass taxes whenever it chose.

Great Britain had found a new way to force its control on the colonies. And the Boston colonists found ways to resist the new laws in response. The rest of the colonies followed Boston's lead.

The Suspending Act

The Townshend Acts did more than tax the colonies on everyday goods. A part of the law called the Suspending Act also shut down New York's assembly. This was where that colony's laws were made. This extra punishment was directed at New York because New York City had refused to obey the Quartering Act of 1767. This law said colonists had to pay for British soldiers to be fed and housed in the city. The assembly was allowed to meet again once the city started to provide food and shelter to British soldiers.

CHAPTER THREE

United in Opposition

Britain had gotten rid of the Stamp Act. But now the colonists were faced with even more harsh rules under the Townshend Acts. In the past, Parliament had not always made colonists pay the taxes on goods brought into the colonies. It also sometimes ignored the smuggling that allowed ship captains to avoid paying taxes. Great Britain now planned to make the colonists follow its rules.

British soldiers arrived to occupy Boston in 1768.

The British customs officers charged with carrying out these laws soon saw that controlling the colonists would not be easy. Many colonists supported smuggling. They often rioted in support of ship owners when officials discovered ships holding smuggled goods. Like the stamp administrators before them, the lives of customs officials and their families were threatened. Great Britain decided to use force to stop the unrest. A warship was sent to help carry out the Townshend Acts.

Women and Resistance

Colonial women had their own ways of resisting the Townshend Acts and supporting boycotts of British goods. Women stopped making clothing from British cloth. Instead they spun wool from their own sheep and wove their own cloth. This homemade cloth became known as homespun.

The *Liberty* Is Seized

John Hancock was a rich Boston merchant who supported the Sons of Liberty. Customs officials

Colonial women spun their own cloth to avoid using imported British goods.

believed one of his ships, the *Liberty*, was smuggling goods. The British towed the *Liberty* away into the harbor in June 1768. Word of what had happened spread through the town. A mob attacked the customs agents at the harbor. They then went to the homes of two others and smashed their windows. The crowds took one of the customs officer's boats and dragged it to Boston Common. There they set it on fire.

Great Britain decided to send more soldiers to Boston to end colonial resistance. Seven British warships with soldiers on board arrived in Boston on

Made in America

Boycotting British goods actually caused positive changes for the colonies in some ways. It forced them to develop their own manufacturing. Glass, paper, and shoes were some of the things the colonies started producing "at home." These items were less expensive when made in the colonies. Colonial factories also provided much-needed jobs for colonial citizens.

October 1, 1768. Two more groups of soldiers arrived soon after.

Resentment, Not Respect

Instead of peace, the soldiers brought more trouble to the streets of Boston. Fights between soldiers and citizens became common. It was one such fight that may have led to the Boston Massacre. Workers at a local business made fun of a soldier passing by on March 2, 1770. The soldier and the workers fought. More soldiers arrived and began beating workers with clubs. More fights broke out the next day, a Saturday. By Monday small groups of men had started to form on the streets. Many of Boston's citizens were now ready for a fight.

Colonists often harassed the British officers.

FURTHER EVIDENCE

New taxes and laws created by the British government angered the American colonists. This led in part to the Boston Massacre. Review Chapter Three. Identify its main point and find supporting evidence. Then visit the Web site below to learn more about the ways in which the colonists fought these taxes and laws. Find a quote that supports the chapter's main point with a new piece of evidence.

The Townshend Revenue Act
www.ushistory.org/declaration/related/townshend.htm

CHAPTER FOUR

In Defense of Reason and Justice

As shots rang out on the day of the Boston Massacre, chaos and anger ruled the streets. Colonists were very angry about what had happened. The news spread quickly through town.

Boston slipped into a state of confusion as late Monday night turned into early Tuesday morning. Lieutenant Governor Thomas Hutchinson was called from his home. He ordered Preston and his men to

The Boston Massacre sent Boston into chaos.

return to their barracks. He then went to the Town House, the seat of the local government, to speak to the townspeople. He urged the people to return to their homes. Preston was arrested and the soldiers who had been involved in the shooting turned themselves in to the authorities. All nine were charged with murder.

The Boston Tea Party

A ship called the *Dartmouth* reached Boston on November 28, 1773. More than 1,000 Boston citizens met to object. They did not want the tea on board to be sold in Boston. Taxes would have to be paid on it. Boston citizens dressed as American Indians threw 342 chests of tea into Boston Harbor on December 16. This was more than 92,000 pounds (41,730 kg) of tea, which would be worth more than a million dollars today. No one was ever brought to trial for the actions of that night.

Adams and Quincy Defend the Soldiers

The angry citizens of Boston demanded the soldiers be tried for the shootings right away. But Hutchinson and other local officials managed to have the trials delayed until fall. John Adams and

Colonists dressed as American Indians threw boxes of tea overboard during the Boston Tea Party in 1773.

Josiah Quincy were the lawyers for the soldiers. They were determined to make sure the soldiers had a fair trial in spite of the strong public feeling against them.

Preston was tried first. Lawyers called witnesses who said they had heard him shout the order to fire before the victims fell. Others didn't think it was the captain shouting "fire" at all. Quincy and

John Adams

Defending the hated soldiers at the Boston Massacre trial put Adams in a difficult position. He understood the citizens' feelings about the British soldiers. But Adams felt the trials were a chance to show how a fair and reasonable society works. In such a society, a person should be considered innocent until proven guilty. Adams felt the Boston Massacre trials called attention to the rights he believed every human being should have.

Adams called witness after witness who said Preston did not order his men to fire. They used the witnesses to create a picture of panic and confusion. Preston's trial was full of uncertainty. He was found not guilty.

The outcome of Preston's trial made it more difficult for the eight other soldiers to defend themselves in their cases. Many people thought if Preston had not given the order to fire, the soldiers must have done so without orders. If this was true, they were guilty of murder.

Adams felt the soldiers' trials were a chance to show how a fair society works.

Witnesses were called who said the soldiers had harassed the citizens. Quincy and Adams called other witnesses who said the townspeople had threatened the soldiers. They were trying to prove the soldiers had fired in self-defense. Also helping the soldiers' case was the confusion about what exactly happened that night. None of the witnesses could say for sure whether the shouts of "fire" were connected to the actions of the soldiers or to the ringing of the bells.

In the end, six of the eight soldiers were found not guilty. Two were found guilty of manslaughter, or killing someone without meaning to. Their punishment was branding of their thumbs with a hot iron.

EXPLORE ONLINE

Go to the Web site below and look at Paul Revere's engraving of the Boston Massacre. There are several differences between the way the engraving looks and the way the story is told in this book. Can you find three differences? Why do you think Revere chose to show events in this way?

Boston Massacre
www.earlyamerica.com/review/winter96/enlargement.html

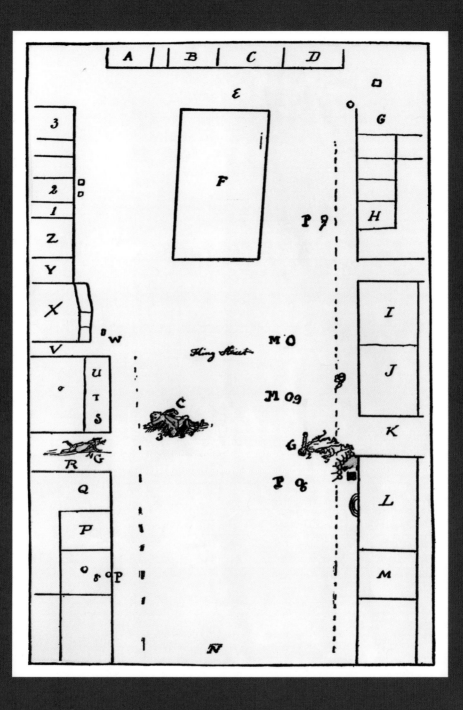

Paul Revere's drawing of the Boston Massacre on King Street was used in the trial of the British soldiers.

CHAPTER FIVE

The Foundations of Independence

A funeral for four of the victims of the Boston Massacre was held on March 8, 1770. They were laid to rest in a single grave. On the other side of the Atlantic Ocean, another important event was taking place. On March 5, the same date as the Boston Massacre, Parliament began to get rid of the Townshend Acts. These laws were part of what caused the Boston Massacre.

Some colonists considered the Boston Massacre to be the first battle of the war.

A woodcut image of the Boston Massacre victims' coffins labeled with their initials.

Fanning the Flames of War

No one on the street on that cold March night knew the colonies would one day declare independence. Angry colonists used what happened that night to argue against Parliament making rules for the American colonies.

The massacre showed how tense the relationship between the colonies and Great Britain was becoming. It would take years to convince colonists to break away. A bloody war would have to be fought to gain independence.

Boston Today

The place where the Boston Massacre happened looks very different today. The Custom House on King Street is long gone. In its place is a high-rise office building. A circle of paving stones marks an area near the spot where the Boston Massacre took place. The actual site is now in the middle of a busy street.

About a mile away in Boston Common stands a monument built in

Lexington and Concord

The first battles of the Revolutionary War took place at Lexington and Concord in 1775. One popular myth about this time is that Paul Revere rode through the countryside shouting, "The British are coming! The British are coming!" But Revere would never have used the word British in this way. The farmers living in the countryside still thought of themselves as British even as war came closer. Revere most likely shouted "the regulars are out!" This meant British soldiers, rather than militia, were coming.

Paul Revere rode through the countryside warning of the British arrival.

1888 to honor the victims of the massacre. On the monument are the words of John Adams, "On that night, the foundation of American independence was laid." Also shown are the words of statesman Daniel Webster, "From that moment we may date the severance of the British Empire."

Responding in Verse to the Boston Massacre

This poem was published in the *Boston Gazette and Country Journal*. Many colonists shared these feelings.

Unhappy Boston! see thy Sons deplore,
Thy hallowe'd Walks besmear'd with guiltless Gore:
. . .
Like fierce Barbarians grinning o'er their Prey,
Approve the Carnage and enjoy the Day.
If scalding drops from Rage from Anguish Wrung
If speechless Sorrows lab'ring for a Tongue.
Or if a weeping World can ought appease
The plaintive Ghosts of Victims such as these;
The Patriot's copious Tears for each are shed,
A glorious Tribute which embalms the Dead.

Source: *"THE BLOODY MASSACRE."*
Boston Gazette and Country Journal. *March 12, 1770. Print.*

Changing Minds

This poem talks about the way many colonists felt about the Boston Massacre. Think about what a British soldier might have to say about the same events. Write a poem that expresses that point of view. How might the soldiers have felt about being surrounded by angry townspeople? What might they have said about being arrested and charged with murder?

IMPORTANT DATES

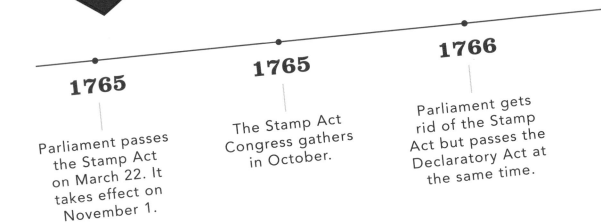

1765

Parliament passes the Stamp Act on March 22. It takes effect on November 1.

1765

The Stamp Act Congress gathers in October.

1766

Parliament gets rid of the Stamp Act but passes the Declaratory Act at the same time.

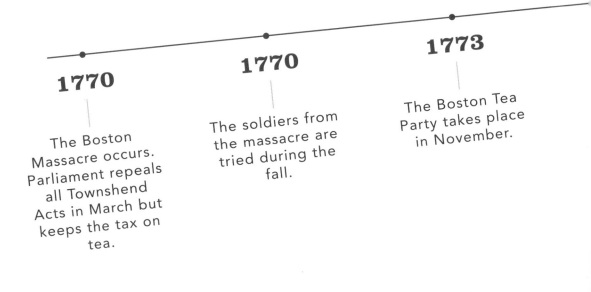

1770

The Boston Massacre occurs. Parliament repeals all Townshend Acts in March but keeps the tax on tea.

1770

The soldiers from the massacre are tried during the fall.

1773

The Boston Tea Party takes place in November.

1767

Parliament passes the Townshend Acts on June 29.

1768

The British government takes John Hancock's ship, *Liberty*, in June.

1768

British soldiers arrive in Boston on October 1.

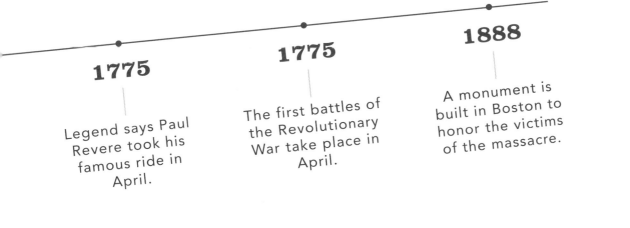

1775

Legend says Paul Revere took his famous ride in April.

1775

The first battles of the Revolutionary War take place in April.

1888

A monument is built in Boston to honor the victims of the massacre.

Take a Stand

This book discusses the relationship between British soldiers and the citizens of Boston during the time leading up to the Revolutionary War. Choose a position on the soldiers' actions. Write a short essay detailing your opinion, the reasons for your opinion, and some facts and details supporting your view.

You Are There

Imagine you are one of the citizens in the mob surrounding the British soldiers. Write 300 words describing your experiences. What is it like to try to move through the crowded streets full of angry citizens? What do you hear as the crowd grows more angry?

Why Do I Care?

The Boston Massacre may have happened long ago, but it still has connections to our lives today. Think of two or three ways the subject of this book connects to your life. For instance, perhaps you sometimes become angry or frustrated when you do not have a say in the rules at home or at school. How have you resolved these kinds of conflicts? How might you resolve them differently?

Tell the Tale

This book discusses how Great Britain angered the American colonists when they imposed "taxation without representation." Write 200 words that tell the true tale of how the colonists felt about these actions. Be sure to set the scene, develop a sequence of events, and offer a conclusion.

GLOSSARY

apprentice
a person who learns a trade by working with a skilled person

barracks
housing for soldiers

bayonet
a weapon like a dagger made to fit on the end of a rifle

brand
a mark put on criminals with a hot iron

effigy
a dummy of a hated person

homespun
homemade cloth

manslaughter
killing someone without meaning to

obituary
a notice of a person's death, usually with some biographical information

smuggle
to bring goods into a country illegally

LEARN MORE

Books

Elston, Heidi M.D. *John Adams.* Edina, MN: ABDO
Publishing Company, 2009.

Fradin, Dennis Brindell. *The Boston Massacre.*
Tarrytown: Marshall Cavendish Benchmark, 2009.

Harness, Cheryl. *The Revolutionary John Adams.*
Washington, DC: National Geographic, 2003.

Web Links

To learn more about the Boston Massacre,
visit ABDO Publishing Company online at
www.abdopublishing.com. Web sites about the
Boston Massacre are featured on our Book Links page.
These links are routinely monitored and updated to
provide the most current information available.
Visit **www.mycorelibrary.com** for free additional tools
for teachers and students.

INDEX

ABOUT THE AUTHOR

Marylou Morano Kjelle is a college professor, freelance writer, and the author of over 40 books for young people. She has a special interest in writing about American history.